It's Taken Me All of My Life

to Find Myself

Assorted Musings of My Lifelong Journey to Self-Discovery, Self-Healing, and Self-Love

Dorothy L. Griggs

Griggs Publishing

Chicago

Griggs Publishing

P.O. Box 3464

Oak Park, IL 60303-3464

ISBN: 0-692-73375-2

ISBN-13: 978-0-692-73375-2

Library of Congress Control Number: 2016909647

Author Photo by Jeff Carrion/DePaul University

This one's for you, grandma.

.

Contents

Acknowledgments

To list individual names would undoubtedly lead to regrettable oversights. So I would like to simply thank everyone who support my work by listening to me, believing in me, encouraging me with your enthusiasm and heartfelt words, and sharing in my belief that the work I do is important and still very much needed. You know who you are – Thank You!

Introduction

"You write in order to change the world, knowing perfectly well that you probably can't, but also knowing that literature is indispensable to the world…The world changes according to the way people see it, and if you alter, even by a millimeter, the way people look at reality, then you can change it."

— James Baldwin

Racism and colorism—two sides of the same American coin. A currency that buys marginalization, violence, and systemic oppression on the one side; flip it over to reveal shame, black-on-black violence, and dispiritedness on the other.

The constant stream of dismissive and dehumanizing messages which blacks have been subjected to since arriving in this country has become so deeply entrenched in the black psyche that we have subconsciously internalized the loathing and hatred directed at us. And, if we are not careful and ever vigilant, this loathing and hatred will distort and morph into *self*-loathing and *self*-hatred, resulting in us thinking and behaving in ways that lend credence to the messages of our oppressors, who then look at us, point, and smugly state, "See, I told you so."

This self-hatred can permeate every fiber of our being and manifest itself in how we treat ourselves, how we talk about ourselves, and how we treat and talk about one another. It becomes evident in the value we place on our lives and the lives of our brothers and sisters. The self-loathing may manifest itself in a bleak vision for the future and a sense of being damned at birth. And when people believe that they are indeed damned and have no real chance at succeeding in life, the attitude that may logically follow is WTF! And when one's attitude is WTF...well, pick up a newspaper, any paper, digital or otherwise.

Viewed in this light, it is easy to see that racism does not just hurt the people whom it is directed toward, but it damages society as a whole by denying groups of people their right to life, liberty, and freedom, while expecting them to be happy and carefree, obedient, and productive citizens. America, you cannot have your cake and eat it, too.

In the intersectionality of the myriad aspects of my life, racism and colorism have been the two separate yet intricately woven fabrics that I have struggled to render transparent in an attempt to better understand my identity as a black woman in America. These loaded identifiers were not of my own choosing but ones that society draped upon my head and shoulders at birth, leaving me to either suffocate beneath their oppressive weight or to square my shoulders, plant my feet, and try to make sense of this moment in history where I find myself. I have chosen to do the latter.

I want to believe that most educated people now understand that race is a social construct—humanity's attempt to categorize people by grouping them based on certain similarities. Racism is humanity's further attempt to create a hierarchy among the categories of race. And in this human-created hierarchy, blacks have historically not fared well.

One of the subversive weapons of war—and racism is viewed by blacks as a war on black lives—has been to divide and conquer, pitting blacks against one another by creating yet another hierarchical system within the black race using what initially appears to be the arbitrary criteria of skin color, hair texture, and facial features, giving birth to the bastard child we now refer to as colorism, but in fact serves to further the claim of white superiority.

Alice Walker, the Pulitzer Prize–winning writer and activist, coined the term *colorism* to describe the internalized bias and favor for light skin, European features, and "good" hair.

Living while being silently and constantly judged, not based on my actions or character, but on the irrelevancy of my physical attributes, both by the white community and within my own black community, can be a source of anger, anguish, confusion, and lead to a sense of being lost within oneself.

But in America that's what we do—we persecute those who are different from us in order to feel better about ourselves. Enter the new kids on the block. They change their names, straighten their hair, possibly have a little nip and tuck performed on the eyes and the nose, and are slowly assimilated and accepted into the majority culture. Now America loves them. She loves their food, she wants to learn their language, their kids can play together, and life is good! Then more new, but different kids move onto the block, and the cycle begins anew, with some of those same kids who themselves were persecuted not so long ago now becoming the persecutors.

But here's the thing, America. Black folk and other people of color can only assimilate so much. I can attempt to master your language, cook foreign cuisine like master chefs, sing along to country music, binge watch all of the episodes of *Downton Abbey* in one sitting, but when I walk down the street, there is no mistaking me. Yep, I'm Black! And despite the constant bombardment of messages to the contrary, I know that I am capable and beautiful.

So I finally figured that since I would never be fully accepted by white America, I had better get on with the business of learning how to fully love my Black American self. But even that proved to be tricky, as some black folks don't care much for me either. My skin is too dark. My hair is too kinky. My laugh is too loud. What's a girl to do?

It's taken me a long time, a lifetime really, but I finally figured it out. Just be me. That's all. Just live my life being my best authentic self, regardless of all of the external noise and confusion out there about who others think I am, and how others think I should think and behave.

Growing up as a shy introvert, I have journeyed through life travelling amidst crowds but always feeling a little removed, a little closer to the periphery of life, watching, observing, trying to make sense of things that were served up as absolute truths, some of which were even codified into laws, but which I could not reconcile in my mind or heart as such.

In this sense, I have always been an unwitting researcher, with myself at the center of my inquiry. I have bravely shown up and dared to look at the unexamined areas of my life. I have found pain and clarity, but ultimately, I have found peace. It seems fitting that life has led me to take up pen and paper and record some of the lessons and observations of this journey for others who, like me, dare to go below the surface and attempt to make meaning of their lives and, in the process, discover their authentic selves.

This book is an auto-ethnographic examination of my life and includes journal entries, essays, and thoughts that I have jotted down on stray pieces of paper over the years. Its goal is to examine my life by using the intellectual traditions of critical race theory, analytic philosophy, and psychoanalysis to illuminate the ontological and epistemological trajectory of my life—or stated another way, what I see as my reality and how I learn about my world.

It is my desire that this book find its way into classrooms, boardrooms, libraries, bookstores, book clubs, personal libraries—any and everywhere people are engaged in the act of consciously seeking to better understand themselves and the world in which they live.

In the process of unpacking some aspects of my life's story, hopefully I can in some small way help others in their personal journeys toward self-discovery, self-healing, and self-love.

Reflection on and contemplation of one's life journey are essential to meaning making. Living consciously is the pathway to disrupting thoughts and behaviors that characterize both the oppressor and the oppressed. Don't despair if you don't have all of the answers. Being brave enough to ask the questions that can take you beneath the pat, neat narrative of our country is an important first step. From there, stay curious and awake.

Living consciously is something that each of us can do. We will never be perfect people, but all that we can do is ALL that we can do. Then sit back and watch as the universe rises up to do that which humans cannot.

What's It All About?

"Rather than love, than money, than fame, give me truth."

— Henry David Thoreau, *Walden*

All of us have experienced the miracle of birth. All of us will also at some point come to the realization that just as we were born, one day we will surely die. In between the bookends of birth and death, we attempt to fashion a life for ourselves. And along the way, we may find ourselves asking, "What is this life all about?"

People use many means to try and find the answers to this age-old question. Some view religion as the key to unlock the answers. Others turn to drugs to expand and free their minds—or at the very least, numb them to the uncertainty of their existence. Many look to nature for answers. Others turn within. There are as many paths to discovering the meaning of one's life as there are individuals. Part of the journey of life is finding a path of discovery that is right for you based on who you are seeking to become.

Throughout this journey, absolute answers to many of life's deepest mysteries may continue to elude us while we are bound to our earthly bodies. But just because we do not have all of the answers, we should not be fooled into believing that there is no rhyme or reason, order, or justice to our universe. I believe the way many people choose to live their lives depends, in part, on what they believe will happen to them after they die. Regardless of one's personal motivation, this present moment in time is all that is, but there are many more moments to come that no one can foresee or predict, so we would all be wise to try and leave kindness and goodness in our wake.

I grew up in a very religious household. My mother unfailingly took my siblings and me to small storefront Pentecostal churches where holy rollers were a common sight and the choirs were so phenomenal that even a quiet, reserved kid such as myself was frequently fearful that the next organ shrill accompanied by the powerful unified voices of the choir would cause me to be hit by the Holy Ghost, and have me running up the aisles doing the holy dance and speaking in tongues. I was thankful that it never happened, but to this day, it is not the sermons that I recall from those days of old, but rather those old spirituals and gospel songs that found a home in the depths of my soul and rise up unexpectedly to strengthen and soothe me during life's challenging times.

While drugs and alcohol were prevalent in inner-city Detroit where I grew up, and smoking pot and drinking beer was a rite of passage—yes, I did inhale—fear and the stark realities of addiction that I witnessed in family members and friends, led me to seek other means to having both mind-expanding experiences and escaping the harsh realities of growing up poor. Additionally, it was clear to me early on that my survival of both an impoverished city and a racist nation required that I not go through life with muted senses, but to remain alert and vigilant to what I could see as well as what I could intuit.

In this chapter of my life, I find myself seeking out the incomprehensible beauty of nature and turning inward when contemplating the question, "What's it all about?" Nature and reflection are available to all and require nothing from us but the desire to live consciously. Nature does not further separate us by requiring us to choose sides. It is neutral and available to us all, though admittedly not in the same amount or to the same degree. But even for city dwellers who are assaulted by dirty air, noise pollution as well as visual overload, a slice of sky between towering high rises is always available to us as a reminder to press the pause button of our lives, slow down, and actually give some thought to this life we are living.

Silence and meditation can slow our breath and calm our minds and allow us, even when in the throes of a personal storm, to retreat inward to a place where important answers lie. That inner, quiet space is the only space that we have sovereign rule over and that cannot be sullied by the external world—unless we allow it to enter. It is a space that is accessible at any time, in any environment, under any circumstance. It is our own private oasis, and its beauty is only limited by our imagination and our ability to conceive and believe.

Much in the same way that we have to schedule exercise to remain physically healthy because today's modern world has most of us seated in front of a computer monitor for most of our waking hours, it is imperative that we also schedule time to sit in quiet reflection because those quiet moments that were once a natural part of our lives are also now in short supply.

But life lived with eyes wide open can be tough to handle some days. As advanced and "civilized" as we have become, it seems that on certain important issues we took a wrong turn and have yet to figure out how to get back on path. The degree of greed, violence, and hatred in the world can leave us with a feeling of hopelessness, but love, kindness, grace, and hope keeps lifting us up out of the depths of our despair.

I hope that we—the individuals who make up our larger communities of neighborhoods, states, nations, and countries—obtain the necessary intelligence and courage to start aggressively self-correcting and getting ourselves on the right path. I hope that as we continue to make advancements in our knowledge, tools, and technology, we include advancements in the care of our fellow human beings. Awareness of our interconnectedness could aid us in this quest as we move forward. If you have ever been truly in need, you already intimately understand this interconnectedness to be true. Money, fame, and fortune do not exempt any of us from the realities of life. So on our quest to amass all of the latest and greatest, we should also try to connect with our spirit and live a life of integrity, compassion, empathy, and honor. The power to do so is within each one of us, regardless of our external circumstances.

At some point in our adult lives, we have to make a conscious decision about the lives we are living and the person we are becoming. The words that we say, the acts that we perform, and even our private thoughts that we never give voice to, help mold us into who we are. And as long as we are alive, we are in a constant state of becoming. So we each need to decide for ourselves what it is we are becoming, what we are in pursuit of during this journey called Life.

We live in a world where many people go along to get along. Belonging is such a fundamental, basic human need that many people give up the true essence of themselves just so that they can fit in. I have never been one to fit neatly into any of the boxes prescribed by society for someone like me. So I don't try to wedge myself into the boxes. I consider this to be an admirable trait of mine, marching to my own beat, but it has also led to feeling misunderstood a lot. People want others to fit in a box. It prevents them from having to do the actual work of getting to know the individual.

There are certain things that we all take for granted —that the planets will continue to revolve around the sun, that the sun will come out tomorrow—hell, there's even a song that proclaims it to be so—and that humankind will keep evolving steadily forward and onward.

But there is now indisputable proof that the polar ice caps are melting, and homelessness in our country has gone from being an anomaly to a commonplace occurrence that is witnessed daily in urban America, as is the deaths by gunfire of so many of our children. It might be time for us to not take so many things for granted and to start assessing what's really going on, but more specifically, to examine the role that we each are playing in creating and shaping our world, and whether we are, in fact, actually evolving into better humans or devolving into lesser beings.

In the middle of all of this rampant ignorance, apathy, violence, and confusion, where does one turn to find the tribe of conscious thinkers, that group of individuals who have succeeded in rising above the mire? Politics? Religion? The justice system? Academia? The sciences?

It seems logical that we would turn to our smartest, brightest, and most morally evolved men and women. Right? Well, the problem with that thinking is that if we take these smart/evolved/morally enlightened individuals in whom we place absolute faith and our collective hope and trust, we will find numerous examples of where that trust has been betrayed, where these superior human beings have stumbled and fallen off the pedestal that we placed them on. Politicians succumb to greed and line their pockets with cash while closing schools in urban communities. Countless wars have been fought in the name of religion, and the Holy Word has been used to justify some of the world's most horrific atrocities. Our justice system packs our prisons with countless black and brown bodies, in many ways reminiscent of the black and brown bodies packed in the hull of slave ships, while affluent whites are given a slap on the wrist for similar or greater crimes. In the world of education, educators fill our heads with teachings of their philosophers, innovators, artists, and heroes with scarce mention of our own. History has shown where scientists possessed great knowledge and curious minds but lacked the moral compass that would have prevented them from turning unsuspecting people into human guinea pigs.

The very people who we are taught to look up to— our leaders, our visionaries, our people of faith, our healers, our protectors—even they succumb to greed, hatred, pride, envy, and ignorance.

December 2013

When my boys were young, I taught them that we all make mistakes because we are human and thus imperfect. I also taught them that once they realized their mistake, if they honestly felt remorseful, then they must apologize. But more important than the apology, they must then do all within their power to right their wrong. Then, if they repeat the same misdeed, it is apparent that their apology was not sincere.

This is not an indictment of all our leaders because that would be generalizing and stereotyping the many based on the behavior of the few, but the mere fact that someone has reached a level in society that we hold in esteem is not, in and of itself, indicative of that individual's good character. That is to say that we must try to ascertain, on a person-by-person basis, whether or not an individual is worthy of our trust, worthy of our respect, worthy of us following his or her teachings.

We must learn to avoid being lulled into compliance by someone's social status without taking the time to determine whether the individual is healthy and whole and coming from a place of light and love versus a place that is fearful and fractured.

There is no one place where you can go, no one group of people who you can turn to and implicitly trust to do the right thing every time. We are all human and therefore flawed. It matters little that someone wears a badge, a collar, or a judicial robe, if someone has taken the Hippocratic oath or is in any of the myriad positions of leadership and power. That person is subjected to the same temptations and limited, narrow thinking of those with less education, and fewer privileges and opportunities. The measure of a person should not be predicated on the answers to questions about what they do and how much they make, but rather on harder questions. *Who are you? What is important in your life? What are you fighting for?* The questions worth asking are those which will help to determine whether the individual is <u>living</u> a life that embodies honor, a life that is worthy of respect and emulation.

Much has been written lately about people taking orders from authority figures to commit harmful acts to others and feeling absolved from any sense of remorse or responsibility for their actions. Do not go through life blindly following orders.

This then brings us to the inevitable question of whom we should turn to for guidance, if not the people that *we ourselves* have elevated to positions of power and influence. Am I proposing that we turn away and shun the leaders of our nation? No, not at all. I am simply proposing that we all learn to trust ourselves a little bit more. Trust that inner voice that tells us right from wrong, even though we sometimes choose to ignore it. Start believing more in the things that you feel —your gut, your sixth sense, your intuition, those hairs that rise on the back of your neck, that tingle down your spine. Whatever it is, and whatever you choose to call it —it is there for you to use along with your logic and other five senses to help you to make sense of your world.

I believe that we are each equipped with an internal navigation system that is designed to help us plot a more fluid course through life. Trust the years that you have been on this planet and the countless lessons that life has offered you. Even if you have not had the opportunity to achieve higher education, trust that there are many sources through which you can obtain knowledge and wisdom. Trust the connection with the spirits and souls of your departed ancestors. Become a truth seeker. Stop blindly accepting information without first thinking about it from many different perspectives. You will encounter lots of different teachers in this journey, but your body is your first and last teacher, trust your body. Stop stifling what it is trying to tell you. Turn within, and learn to trust yourself.

We humans can sometimes be such nonsensical people. We do things that don't make sense. We say things that don't make sense. We think things that do not make sense. I don't know how we got here. When will we learn how to be noble during good times as well as bad? What are we waiting for? Whom are we waiting for? A hero to come and save us? When will we understand that our individual actions have a ripple effect that goes out into the world but eventually comes back like the waves of the ocean?

As bleak as the world may sometimes seem, I do still have hope for humankind. I know that a lot of other people actually care as well but feel that the problems are too big and insurmountable. One sure road to the failure and demise of us all is for the well intended to do nothing.

Allow yourself to be inconvenienced. Disrupt your default mode and actually start thinking about what you are thinking. Think about why you do what you do and why you say the things that you say. Disrupting your default mode will require you to do things differently from how you've always done them in the past. It will require you to step outside of your comfort zone and behave in ways that may cause others to view you in a different light, to think of you as acting differently, and possibly no longer one of them. Living consciously will require you to have the courage to do what feels right in your soul instead of waiting for someone else to handle the problems that you see before you or worse, waiting on someone else to give you permission to act from your heart.

Ways to Disrupt Your Default Mode:

- ➢ Examine your life.
- ➢ Examine your heart.
- ➢ Be wary of those who claim to have all the answers.
- ➢ Ask yourself, "Why am I here?"
- ➢ What are some valuable life lessons you've obtained thus far in your journey?
- ➢ What virtues are important for you to live, to instill in your children?
- ➢ What does happiness look like?
- ➢ What does love feel like?
- ➢ Are you on path to your greater self?

Am I Really Who You Say I Am?

"No one is born hating another person because of the colour of his skin or his background or his religion. People must learn to hate, and if they can learn to hate, they can be taught to love, for love comes more naturally to the human heart than its opposite."

— Nelson Mandela

I am a thinker, a writer, and crier. Being of a sensitive nature, I find that I tend to cry a lot—not necessarily about the conditions of my personal life but about the state of our collective human condition. I may present as someone who is shy, and some people who meet me might think that I am somewhat aloof. And while I am admittedly somewhat shy, I am not what I would consider to be aloof. Rather, I find that I am very susceptible to other people's energy, some of which can be quite lovely and energizing, or lovely and soothing to be around. Other people's energy, however, can feel toxic, abrasive, or insincere, leaving me feeling anxious, agitated, drained, or emotionally under siege. So I have learned to be mindful of the company that I keep, and also mindful of how I expend my energy, choosing to use it for positive endeavors, since there is a limited amount of energy that I have at my disposal each day—which is true for all of us.

As much as I complain about my propensity for crying, I am grateful that my body knows how to care for my soul. And if you are reading this, I ask that you consider crying as a method of allowing your soul to unburden itself of our cumulative earthly pain. This natural method of relief is so much healthier for us all than taking that negative energy that needs to be expelled and releasing it in a torrent of yet more physical pain and emotional human suffering. And once your soul has been freed of some of the weight of the pent-up pain, sadness, and violence that is rampant in our modern world, I ask that you seek some action that you as an individual can take to help ease our collective suffering.

As the youngest of seven children and the third in a pair of stair steps (siblings born less than a year apart), I grew up in a community where most everyone had a nickname. My brother and sister, the other stairs in the stair steps, have the given names Brian and Annette, but we were routinely called by our nicknames: Peter, Dee Dee, and me, Doe Doe. Oftentimes, the names were run together so that there was no distinguishing one from the other, as if we were a single entity:PeterDeeDeeDoeDoe. When my mom said it that way though, it usually meant that we three were in trouble!

My only association with this nickname that I had been given was the dodo bird. The dodo bird is a big, flightless, trusting bird whose too-small wings prevented it from flying. Correction: The dodo bird *was* a big flightless bird whose trust in humans led to its extinction. Most people's understanding of the dodo bird is that it was also clumsy and dumb. Now, granted, I grew up with long limbs that sometimes seemed disconnected from their command center, and I too was born with a trusting heart, but the secret fear that lurked in my heart was that others thought that I, much like the bird, was also dumb.

For many years I accepted this nickname without question. Hell, I even created a way for myself and others to spell it, adding an *e* at the end of each *do*, hoping to place *some* distance between me and that unfortunate bird but mainly to prevent people from mistakenly pronouncing my name as the word that rhymes with, and has the same meaning as, poo.

As I grew older, I became acutely self-conscious about my name and, not so surprisingly, self-conscious about myself. Who gave me this name? I inquired again and again of my mom and older siblings. And, more importantly, why? My anger was stoked anew each time some cute boy asked me that dreaded, loaded question: "Hey, what's your name?" *Dorothy* conjured up images of an old lady or, conversely, visions of me skipping down a yellow-brick road, but what was my alternative?

I felt that my fate was sealed, and it wasn't until my favorite cousin informed me that his mom (the cool and jazzy aunt) told him that she thought that I was refined.

Refined? Whoa! I instantly liked the word and what it represented. And yet, my immediate response was "No, she must have meant Toni," referring to my older sibling who I thought not only had *the* best name but who also did not have a silly nickname to contend with.

"No, she meant you," he replied assuredly and continued with our conversation. What he said next, I didn't hear because time actually stood still. *Refined.* The word echoed in my head. It represented the opposite end of the spectrum of what I was being called on a daily basis. I remember sitting back and thinking, *Can I really be this other, refined person that my aunt sees in me, and no longer surrender to the self-eroding, self-effacing image of myself as clumsy and dumb?*

That conversation with my cousin marked the moment when I realized that my identity was not static, and that even people from the same group, in this case my family, saw me differently. I then reasoned that if everyone saw me differently, then why should I not choose the version that I liked best? Soon after that conversation, I begin insisting that people refer to me by my given name. I still thought it sounded old, but given the alternative, it was starting to sound pretty good.

Over an amazingly short period of time, people quickly fell in line and began to understand that if they wanted to converse with me or to get my attention, they had to refer to me by my given name. By simply changing what I allowed people to call me I began, for the very first time, to see new possibilities for myself.

This experience further taught me that I am really the only one qualified to define me, and that as I change and evolve, I need to be certain that my identity is

21

always of my own choosing, regardless of the environment I find myself, or the people whose company I choose to keep. It is not always easy to do, but it is vital to my mental, emotional, and spiritual health to stay true to the best version of myself that I am striving to become.

When I was growing up, family and friends referred to my maternal grandmother as *Mammy*— no doubt a throwback to what she had been called by her employers whose homes she worked in and whose children she cared for. I can never know the intonation of that loaded word from my grandmother's employers' lips, but when uttered by family members, there was no mistaking that it was spoken as a term of endearment, much in the way that some black folks use the term *nigga*—not to be confused with *nigger*, as traditionally spoken with hatred and contempt by white folks.

Blacks took a word spoken with hatred and intended to demean, degrade, and destroy, and refashioned it to mean affection and brotherhood. Our creativeness and resourcefulness have always aided in our very survival in this country.

As an adult, I made the conscious decision to no longer refer to my grandmother as *Mammy* nor refer to blacks as *niggas* though, again, I do understand the context in which those terms are used by black folk. And to those white people who don't understand why they should not use the word— you had your turn at the word already, and the damage is done. The word coming from your lips will forever draw into question the meaning with which you are imbuing the word. You could mean it playfully, seeing it as an easy way to earn street cred, or you could speak it with the vitriol used by your ancestors. That ambiguity will always be in question and can never be overcome.

A white acquaintance of mine likes to regale me with stories of her *redneck* brother. One day as she started in with yet another story about her *redneck* brother, I couldn't contain myself and interrupted by blurting out, "What does that *mean*?!" I explained to her when I hear the word *redneck*, I automatically think of someone who is bigoted and hateful, and who possibly has a starched white robe at the ready. She stared at me, mouth agape.

"No! No! It's a term of endearment!" she declared and proceeded to speak about said brother in lavishly glowing terms, presumably to help me better understand that all this time she had not been slyly boasting about how backward thinking her brother was.

These stories help to illustrate that the names you call a person or people matters. Which leads to something else I've been pondering. When did people of color go from being called "minorities" to being called "marginalized"? Was it when whites realized that they themselves would soon numerically become the minority?

Now, blacks are referred to as marginalized— marginalized men and women, marginalized students, marginalized children. I chafe at this term in much the same way I chafed at being called Doe Doe. It again feels like one more way to separate blacks from whites, to metaphorically place one race above the other, to use words to continue the perpetuation of the myth that the white race is superior.

Once during a class, we students were asked to list words that defined us. A black woman whose wisdom and insightfulness I have great respect for stated, "I am a marginalized black woman." Hearing her state this so matter-of-factly left me feeling unsettled. Here, this beautiful, intelligent black woman was calling herself marginalized, and I couldn't help but wonder why she would accept that as part of her identity. And if she must, then instead of saying, "marginalized black woman," state more correctly, "a black woman who is marginalized." See the difference? It's slight, but its effects are subtly and stealthily powerful. *Marginalize* is a verb. It is an action word, not an adjective. Instead of referring to marginalization as some type of inherent characteristic, the rewording of the sentence clearly illustrates that the marginalization is coming from an outside force. You are being acted upon by marginalizers.

Is that a word—*marginalizers*? Who makes up these committees who dictate what people should be called? How come white people don't have a name? Should we refer to white people as *marginalizers*? Would that be accurate and appropriate? Would it be kind? Would it be fair? I don't think that *marginalizer is* a word, but it serves to illustrate my point that this phenomenon of marginalization is not happening in a vacuum. It is not happening by something "out there," some unseen, mysterious force. No. It is happening every day by ordinary white men and women who look the other way and choose to remain silent, who laugh at the dehumanizing jokes, who hire and promote only people who look like them, who socialize only with people who look like them, who vote for a man who no one can deny is a bully (while being mortified and stupefied by the escalation of bullying and killings that are happening in our schools by our children). It is in the small day-to-day details that the marginalization and dehumanization takes place. Constantly naming and calling out the oppressed puts the spotlight on them instead of on the oppressors.

Even today most African Americans will acknowledge that their ancestors were highly likely to have been slaves, even while clinging tightly to the hope that their keen noses, lighter skin, or thin lips are the result of Native American ancestry, which in some cases it actually is. This consensual intermixing of the races is naturally preferable to the thought that their ancestors were brutalized and raped by the white slave owners. Thanks to science and technology, African Americans are now able to reconstruct our genealogy and reclaim the knowledge that was stolen from us.

While blacks readily acknowledge that slavery is undoubtedly a part of our heritage, few whites will lay claim to the fact that their ancestors were slave owners. Logic dictates that there could not have been the one without the other.

2000

Does the way America currently teaches our black youth (males in particular) about slavery instill in them the need to become warriors rather than intellectuals?

Before I began to share with you anything about who I am, no doubt you had already formed some loose impressions about who you thought I was based on the title of the book and the photographs on the covers. I have come to understand that there will always be assumptions made. That is just a fact of life.

When most people talk about themselves, they only speak of their external self. We have been conditioned to identify with our accomplishments, which then translate into the stuff that we are able to purchase because of our accomplishments, which then become status symbols that we use to show the world how successful, important, and accomplished we are. But is this who we really are? Are we simply the measure of our stuff?

I have learned to become personally acquainted with the invisible aspect of myself—a self that knows no gender, no race, no religion, and no allegiance to any place on this planet. This invisible self is as free and pure as my creator. Some refer to this invisible self as the soul, but what you choose to call it is not important. What I sincerely believe is important is the need to get in touch with this invisible you—the you that lives below the surface. This invisible self is often forgotten as we grow into adulthood. This invisible part of me is the part that has taken me all of my life to find. This is where the essence of who I truly am resides; thus, this is where my focus needs to be. Here, within, is where the work needs to take place to allow me to continue to evolve into the person I desire to be.

Sometimes as we are going about our lives, we may experience a vague awareness of our invisible selves. I liken it to walking down the street, your mind consumed with a million thoughts, when you suddenly look up and catch a glimpse of your reflection in a plate-glass window. It is so unexpected and fleeting that you find yourself asking, "Was that me?" This is how it can feel when you awaken to the invisible intelligence housed within your physical body. You may hear it whispering to you answers to questions that you have been seeking, and you may find yourself asking, "Is that me?"

Throughout my life I have spent a lot of time inside my head, thinking about the curious inconsistencies of life, things that happen with great certainty but do not make any sense. As a result, I have learned to analyze my life and my environment and the people within it with a conscious, critical eye. That ability may possibly have been born the day that I learned that my aunt thought of me as refined, but I have learned to strengthen it as a means of survival because the forces that seek to diminish my humanity and turn me back into a self-loathing twelve year old are ever present, as in the time a white female college professor asserted in front of my predominately white class, "You people can only have what we allow you to have." I was mortified and humiliated, and I felt a deep sense of shame. School suddenly lost its luster, and it took me many years before I was to return to try again at a different place of higher learning, or to be able to speak aloud my experiences of that day. It made me think of the misplaced shame that rape victims feel that causes them to remain silent.

But when my son came home from elementary school after a day of learning about slavery from his white teacher and informed me that he no longer wanted to be an African American, I knew in that moment that I had to become even more vigilant and acutely aware of subversive messages from alleged trusted sources that were penetrating the young minds of my children.

We all have aspects of our identity that we carry around that are not of our making. Claim your identity, and let the world know who you are. Protect your children from those who would break their young spirits. Maybe black parents should be the ones to first tell our children of this sordid chapter of American history and of our ancestors' arrival to this country. We can offer a more balanced telling of the history and not paint blacks as creatures to be pitied and the white man as our savior. Though as painful as it will assuredly be for us to disrupt their innocence so young, if we tell our own stories of our painful past, we at least get to counter the pain and confusion that they will undoubtedly experience with the comfort of our loving embrace and words of love, strength, pride, grit, and faith, and in the process, eliminate the feeling of shame that the telling of our history invokes when delivered by those without much regard or awareness of the damage they may be inflicting to the young black psyche.

November 3, 2011

There is no cause to be ashamed of the past. Talk about it, understand how it has seeped into the present and use that knowledge to take control of your future.

Crumbs Along the Pathway:

- ➢ Be mindful of what you call others and what you allow others to call you.
- ➢ Unpack and examine any discord between who you were taught to be versus who you know yourself to be.
- ➢ Unpack and examine what you were taught about how the world works versus what your experiences have shown you firsthand.
- ➢ What Tribe do you belong to?
- ➢ Why these people?
- ➢ Did you choose them or did they choose you?
- ➢ Thinking consciously and critically, would you choose them again?
- ➢ Resist the urge to think of someone who is different as the "Other."
- ➢ Who had the greatest influence on how you feel about yourself?
- ➢ Should their opinion of you outweigh your opinion of yourself?
- ➢ Do you like what you see when you look in the mirror?
- ➢ Does your exterior self jibe with your interior self?
- ➢ Stare deep into your eyes and try to catch a glimpse of your soul.
- ➢ Be willing to declare, "This is who I am."

Remember...Life Is Still a

Beautiful Mystery

"In the silence we listen to ourselves. Then we ask questions of ourselves. We describe ourselves to ourselves, and in the quietude we may even hear the voice of God."

— Maya Angelou, *Rainbow in the Cloud*

So if life is difficult and pain is an inevitable part of the human experience, how then do we hang on and keep the faith when darkness threatens to envelop us, and we can no longer see our way through to the light? I have found that it is during these times that it helps to go within and hold on to what you have learned to be your unassailable truths.

Go within and commune with your spirit. This is a

solitary exercise that will require you to steal some time from your physical pursuits to just be alone with yourself. For some, this simple act of being alone and quiet will prove to be quite challenging because we have come to accept as normal the constant barrage of noise, chaos, strife, and confusion. Understand that it is not. We have come to accept as normal spending the majority of our days sitting before blinking monitors. Understand that it is not. We have come to accept as normal food eaten while in transit that comes pre-made and pre-packaged and whose ingredients and methods of production we are ignorant about. Understand that it is not. Understand that sometimes the quickest way to get to where you are going is to stop and stand still long enough to determine whether you are travelling in the right direction.

Go within and remember when the days were too long, and you didn't think you could make it through whatever your struggle was at that moment in time. Go within and recall the countless times when grace showed up in your life in the exact form and at the precise moment that you needed it. Go within and remember the times that you bore witness to miracles, both big and small. We all have been blessed to witness them, but we may have missed the majesty of the moment by being too consumed with our worries and endless desires.

It is in these times of despair that we must remember that we are here for a purpose and to seek the wisdom of our creator. In a busy, noisy, sometimes dark world, I am reminded of the wisdom of naturalist and poet Loren Eiseley who advised, "In the days of the frost seek a minor sun." That sun can be whatever helps to keep you anchored until you can feel that the earth is once again firmly beneath your feet, until you once again possess the knowingness of your connection to a higher source, a connection to your higher power.

November 2000

> *Today I wanted to write about the pink flower budding in the barren tree beneath my sons' bedroom window that I discovered by chance in the morning as I was opening the blinds. I looked out and there it was—a beacon of hope. It seemed to say to me—it's gonna be okay. And during moments of despair I would go and look for the flower and if it was still there, I knew that all would be okay. As I write this, the flower is still there. A little beaten, having survived a couple of snowy nights. A little withered and faded but like me, still hangin' in there. Thank you, God, for the beautiful pink flower.*

Allow yourself to try your hand at something you've always wanted to do. Try painting or drawing, knitting or quilting, gardening or baking. Learn how to play the flute or the violin, or any other musical instrument that strikes your fancy. Dedicate an afternoon to pulling out and listening to all of those old vinyl albums that are the soundtrack to your life, and let yourself take a fun jaunt down memory lane. Journal about the new discoveries you are making about yourself and your world. Try a form of exercise you've never experimented with before—yoga, Pilates, free weights, kickboxing, or tai chi. Learn to mediate, or become a cloud glazer like me. The possibilities are limitless, but the objective is to simply allow yourself to engage in an activity that makes you joyous. It is not necessary to commit to trying to become an expert but simply to give yourself permission to do something for the sheer pleasure of doing it. The reward will come from mindfully engaging in the activity, which will allow you to unplug, slow down, and breathe.

In our society, we are encouraged to work harder by multitasking, working faster, jumping higher, working longer hours, working through meals, working while on vacation, working while our children are attempting to connect with us. The lists of the ways in which we try to be superhuman are endless. As a result, we are a nation on the verge of a collective mental breakdown. Little is sacred these days. We have veered far from our true north, evidenced by the fact that we have somehow forgotten our responsibility to protect our children and our elders. So while we are all very busy, and we may be accomplishing a lot, many of us are living empty and miserable lives.

As we go about our daily lives we should try and remember our connection to the land. All of us, regardless of our culture, come from people who had a more intimate relationship with Mother Earth. Rekindle your appreciation of the land by planting something in the ground and nurturing it as it grows—a tree, a bush, or a garden. If you do not have access to outdoor land, plant an herb garden in a planter box and place on your windowsill. Buy a houseplant and repot it in a pretty flowerpot of your choosing, which will not only allow you to experience the richness of the soil between your fingers and the sharp fragrant scent of the soil welcoming life, but which will also encourage you to engage in the process of caring for the very things that sustain y*our* life on this planet while simultaneously thrilling your senses with indescribable gifts of beauty and joy. Finding ways to remember and appreciate the goodness and beauty of this planet and your reliance on her will continue to feed your body and spirit.

June 4, 2014

> *It is because of the wind that I am so in love with trees. If trees were static creatures, they would not be able to make my heart soar nor capture my imagination and let me briefly escape the sometimes harsh realities of my earthly existence to soar high to the treetops and accept their invitation to dance.*

It is in the quiet moments that you will be able to discover what is important to you and what the measure of your success will look like. Maybe it is having a lot of advanced degrees, or maybe it's simply being able to get home early enough to cook your family a homemade meal—nothing overly extravagant but made with your hands and made with attention, love, and care. It is important to make, or rather, to *take* these moments of quiet time so that you can define the person that you are becoming. If you do not, others will do it for you, and you will wake up on day, and you may ask yourself, in the words of David Byrne, "Well…how did I get here?"

Ways to Express Gratitude:

➢ Cherish and respect your elders.
➢ Be wary of those who claim they have all the answers.
➢ Champion the youth.
➢ Trust in tomorrow.
➢ Live to make your creator proud.
➢ Meditate.
➢ Pray.
➢ Commune with nature—become a cloud gazer!
➢ Play.
➢ Learn to enjoy spending time alone.
➢ Learn to welcome silence.
➢ Say please and thank you more often.

No One Said It Would Be Easy,

but Sweet Baby Jesus!

"It is easier to build strong children than to repair broken men."

— Frederick Douglass

My grandmother, Elvira Lawson, was born in 1888 in Hawkinsville, Georgia. At the age of nineteen she married nineteen year old Essic Lampkin, and three years later, they moved to the state of Oklahoma, where they resided for fourteen years before moving to Inkster, Michigan, where they lived until my grandmother's passing in 1980. During their seventy-two years of holy matrimony, together they raised nine children, six daughters and three sons. The eldest daughter, Eliza, is my mom.

Upon arriving at my grandparents' home, we were greeted with an explosion of colors, as each year my grandfather, the family gardener, would plant row upon row of flowers where the front lawn had once been. It simultaneously delighted my senses and informed me that it was okay to be different.

Growing up I didn't have a particularly close relationship with my grandmother. Being one of twenty-seven grandchildren, I wonder now if she even knew my name. As a shy child growing up hearing the often-repeated phrase, "Children should be seen and not heard," I had a difficult time making myself heard. I have since mourned the missed opportunities of really getting to know my grandmother while she was alive, but as a child I was content to sit in her kitchen, perched on a high stool, watching the world of grown folks swirl around me as she sat tall and regal, holding court at the kitchen table surrounded by an aura of calmness and love.

Many of our ancestors' voices are silenced forever, but if you listen closely, you may hear their voices or feel their loving presence guiding you, teaching you lessons garnered from their journey with a clarity and wisdom that we cannot yet comprehend.

I first heard my grandmother's voice as a quiet whisper early one morning as I awakened from a dream while pregnant with my first child. Since that day I often sense her loving energy close by, and I am grateful for her continued presence in my life. I have only recently come to realize that I resemble my grandmother, with her thin lips and quiet demeanor.

I have many good memories of those days spent at

my grandparents' home filled with the love of family and the scent of teacakes baking in the oven, not to mention the omnipresent cut-glass bowls of hard candies that have become synonymous with the grandmothers of that generation.

I never witnessed nor heard talk of sadness or grief in that little house in Inkster, Michigan. Yet, the advantages that age, reflection, and hindsight have given me is a deeper knowledge of my history and a better understanding of the times that my grandparents lived through and the struggles that they most assuredly endured. It's funny when looking back over your life the stories that want to make themselves known and the bits of history that want acknowledgment.

Racial injustice has always been an anvil tethered to life as an African American. It was then. It is now. Most people I grew up with always went south to visit their grandparents over summer vacation. I never went south for the summer because my maternal grandparents (I never knew my paternal grandparents) were already firmly ensconced in the north by the time I showed up. Reflecting upon their lives, I often wonder what prompted their move north from Pottawatomie County, Oklahoma, and whether it was in any way connected to one of America's deadliest terrorist acts, the race riots that took place approximately a hundred miles away in 1921 in Tulsa, Oklahoma, where a wealthy black community known as Black Wall Street was burned to the ground by white residents, leaving hundreds of blacks dead, and countless others homeless.

This chapter of American history most people know little to nothing about, but in order to understand where we stand as a nation, we all need to have a clearer understanding of where we come from.

Note to Self

August 20, 2014

Hello Dorothy,

God has given you a gift (your name literally means God's gift). You know in your core that you have something to share, and it is therefore your obligation to rise above your fear of being less than, rise above your fear of not being good enough, rise above your fear of thinking that someone else can do what God put in your heart to do.

As of today, you are making great strides at owning your power and speaking with confidence. This is new, so it's okay if your voice wavers and your eyes tear—it's not a sign of weakness, so release the need to be perfect and know that you will be accepted into people's hearts for precisely the reasons that you fear you are not good enough.

When your time on this planet is done, you want your Father to be pleased.

Live your life from that end goal, and all will be fine.

In love, confidence, and peace. Amen.

Dorothy

When I was a child growing up in the predominately black city of Detroit, Michigan, racism was not something that I ever personally encountered. I do, however, have a vague memory of standing on the porch one night while my dad sat listening to the live radio broadcast of a riot that was taking place in our city. The smoke from the burning buildings filled my nostrils and the night calm was punctured by the sound of sirens and gunshots in the background, making very real the battle that raged literally blocks away. I still felt safe on my daddy's porch, and I thought of racism as some far away, abstract monster, even while being keenly aware of the shotgun propped in the corner directly behind my daddy's chair.

1994

I want to grow a baby in my belly and dreadlocks on my head.

October 1995

Everywhere you look there's a flow of black men heading toward the U.S. Capitol. The few whites are headed away from the Capitol and away from the gathering mass of black men. My husband looks particularly handsome this morning, wearing the African beads I purchased for him in Detroit last weekend. Squeezing our way through the throng of black people, we've gotten as close to the Capitol as we physically can, without doing that, "excuse me, pardon me, excuse me, please" stuff. My first impression is simply, "Wow!"

By the time my first son was born, I unequivocally understood the magnitude of the task I was about to undertake—to raise this little brown bundle of wonderment into an individual who was kind, compassionate, intelligent, and a doer of good deeds. Almost two years later, my second son was born, and the weight of the responsibility I felt at bringing another child into the world was not diminished by having already done it once before.

Seeing the world through the innocent, trusting eyes of my sons, it soon became clear to my husband and me that as our young sons evolved from their little baby powder-scented chubby selves and started toddling through the world, that there would soon come a day that we would have to relinquish them to the larger world. So, in addition to protecting them from the typical dangers inherent in child rearing—sharp corners, stranger danger, and choking hazards—it was also our duty to try and prepare them for the world that lay beyond our front door and the struggles of the time into which they had been born.

October 2000

This is the lesson to take away regardless of how painful it this: Don't allow myself to make the mistake of trying to put a pretty dressing on a painful and ugly truth.

There were many lessons and virtues that I needed to instill in them—ways to distinguish friend from foe; to surround themselves with good people and to choose their friends carefully; to pursue their passions, even if it didn't meet with the approval of others; and to strive to be a source of light and love. The list was/is endless and the responsibility of raising children can often feel overwhelming. But in the recesses of my soul, I have always felt that if I could teach them to become independent thinkers, all of the other things that I desired for them would flow naturally from their ability to objectively and critically analyze their world.

Race relations were seldom discussed in my home. One reason for this, I believe, was that it was a painful and shameful subject. Fast-forward to the present day, and things are starting to shift. Conversations about race now *must* take place in black homes to help black youth understand what forces they are up against when they are walking while black, driving while black, and laughing while black. We now freely speak about the pain and allow it to be expressed with our voices, in our faces, and through our art. But the shame...the shame still binds us.

Much like my son, I too felt shame for being an African American when the class discussion turned to slavery. But unlike him, I chose silence and stuffed the pain and shame deep inside where no one could see. I distinctly remember how the pictures in our history books always made me feel ashamed to be associated with those poor people in those giant slave ships, packed tightly away like sardines. I also experienced what I interpreted as a look of pity from my white classmates as they listened to the same stories, seemingly void of any of the feelings of connection to their slave-owning ancestors, so unlike the connection that blacks felt toward their enslaved ancestors.

As they listened to the story, our story, their pity only heightened my sense of shame. At no time did the educator attempt to draw the white students into the story and help them become aware that some of their ancestors had actually been the perpetrators of the horrific crimes we were reading about, and that all of them were living with the unearned privilege born of those times. It felt as if the textbook writers and the educators wanted to keep a veil of innocence between the white students and their connection to the past, but rip the veil away to display in stark details the suffering of the black slaves.

Blacks will undoubtedly always experience deep emotions when it comes to slavery; shame, however, must cease to be one of them.

The birth of my sons was the spark that ignited the fire within me to try and live a self-actualized life. What better way to teach my sons than to try and embody the lessons and virtues that I hold dear. So at the age of fifty-two, I finally completed my undergraduate degree and went on to obtain my master's degree.

But in addition to pursing higher education as a means to teach and guide my sons, I also knew that my own unexamined life contained a wealth of information, nuggets of hard-won wisdom that I could pass on if I were brave enough to excavate them. This book is an examination of some of those nuggets—or rather, transformative moments in my life—that led me to a deeper understanding of myself and my world, a few of the signposts that shaped me into the woman I am today—the critical thinker that I had to become in order to make sense out of life's curious inconsistencies, including trying to figure out why it is that black folks who have an understanding of the history and genesis of colorism continue to feed the monster instead of starving it to death.

My six siblings and I exhibit skin coloring of at least three distinct shades of brown. My shade falls somewhere in the middle. My brown skin has not afforded me unearned acceptance by white society, and neither has it granted me admiration from shallow black men nor disdain from darker-skinned women.

My hair, however, is decidedly African. The texture is strong and tightly coiled. It had been altered with heat and chemicals for as far back as I can remember. After leaving Detroit and moving to the north side of Chicago, I would take the bus to work each day and be surrounded by Caucasian women whose hair blew in the breeze, something that my chemically processed hair would only do on the day that it was freshly washed and blown out. I wanted my hair to blow in the breeze too, so I started getting up early every morning to wash and blow my hair out. Black women, you already know where this is headed, but to my other readers, black hair that has been chemically altered is not as strong and healthy as hair in its natural state. Continued application of chemicals (including shampoo which can strip the hair of its natural oils) will cause the hair to become dry, damaged, and prone to breakage. That is what I subjected my hair to in the quest to have it look like white women's hair. But *my* hair could not be further from white women's hair, people!

It was during that time that I realized that I had been altering my hair for so long that I no longer even knew its natural color nor remembered its natural texture. After many decades of altering my hair, I made the decision to let it go natural. Now that I am older, my hair is gray or, according to my husband, practically white. The texture is also changing in strange and unexpected ways. With the passage of time, it makes me sad that I didn't appreciate the strength and character of my natural hair earlier. Will I always wear my hair natural? Only time will tell. But whatever I choose, it will now come from a place of self-acceptance and self-love, instead of me trying to be something that I am not.

Once we learn to fully love and accept ourselves, our skin, our hair—whatever color or texture it may be—we can redirect all of the time and energy spent on self-loathing and self-defeating behaviors and use them to deal with the real business of keeping our children safe and making our communities strong.

Eradicating colorism will naturally weaken the grip of racism by depriving it of one of its most important nutrients—our continued ignorance of our individual and collective beauty, intellect, and power.

Transforming From the Inside Out:

- ➢ Who taught you whom to love?
- ➢ Who taught you whom to hate?
- ➢ Who taught you who/what to worship?
- ➢ How are the above three questions manifesting in your life, and are they lessons that you should possibly re-think?
- ➢ Who do you trust?
- ➢ Are they worthy of your trust?
- ➢ Are you travelling on higher ground?
- ➢ Would you make your ancestors proud?
- ➢ As you grow and change, whom might you disappoint?
- ➢ As you grow and change, who may disappoint you?
- ➢ Understand that the truth can be painful.
- ➢ Allow yourself to feel the pain.
- ➢ Forgive yourself for your shortcomings.
- ➢ Forgive others, bless them, and move on if necessary.

Finding Your Voice/Living Your Truth

"Freedom is a beautiful thang!"

— Prince

When faced with information that challenges everything you've believed up until that moment in time, your world may tilt on its axis. The truth is often hard to bear. But it has also been said that the truth will set you free.

It wasn't until I was a young adult working at a large, diverse hospital that I became aware that other people paid a lot of attention and spent a lot of time working to identify people's race, ethnicity, religion, socioeconomic status, and educational level.   In America, it seems that we are not so much interested in the hearts or characters of people but rather whether they belong to our tribe. And if it is apparent that they do not belong to our dominant tribe, which in America is characterized by race, we want to know if they have any other identifiers that match up with our own. The more of these identifiers they possess, the more likely it is that

47

we will accept them as being worthy of our time and energy. The fewer matchups, the less likely that we will make the effort to try to get to know them.

A few years back, as I was solemnly sharing with a coworker a story about a young lady who died after being hit by a tour bus in downtown Chicago, she laughed out loud—a big guffaw. Not exactly the reaction I was expecting. I quickly became irritated and annoyed, and concluded the story by saying how sad it was that this young woman's family had to come from Europe to claim their child.

Upon hearing that, there was a huge perceptible shift in my coworker's disposition, body language, and energy. Suddenly, this was no longer a caricature of a sudden death, but a tragic tale of somebody's child, someone's friend, a human being with hopes and dreams that would never be fulfilled. It was not until it was revealed that this young woman belonged to a tribe that my coworker identified with, did she become deserving of her compassion and respect.

This whole encounter sat uneasy in my soul and begged the question: Do Americans reserve feelings of compassion and empathy only for members of their own tribe? As I've already confessed, I am a crier, so this does not apply to me personally, but the incident made me view racism from a different perspective. I already know that white America primarily chooses members of their own tribe on whom to bestow the resources and opportunities that this nation has to offer; whether this happens consciously or unconsciously is what is in question, the fact that it is happening is not.

But has it gone even deeper than material goods and

wealth and has now sullied our basic humanity? Even as I ask myself the question, I already know that the answer is, sadly, yes. History tells us so. In fact, there are numerous examples in history where people have numbed themselves so that they lack feeling for their fellow human beings. The reasons are as numerous— they can't be bothered, got important things to do; it's too painful, don't want to go there; it benefits them and those of their tribe; it's not happening to them or their loved ones.

And while the world has finally been awakened to the epidemic of killings of unarmed black men, women and children, is it not possible for white America to understand the depth of the pain, rage, and despair that is felt in the black community? Are you not capable of feeling my pain because my skin is not the color of yours? Can you not cry for me? I know when you have chosen sympathy over empathy when I see you glancing at me with sorrowful, pitying eyes. It immediately lets me know that you do not understand because if you did, when I looked into your eyes, I would see a reflection of the pain that is in mine.

The randomness and the senselessness of the killings make them especially haunting. I am a good, kind person. My skin is black. It will always be black; that fact will never change. Something else then must change.

When you witness injustices, don't deny the truth of what you are seeing simply because the offender looks like you or your son or anyone else in your tribe. What fate befalls the victim is apparent, but not all of the consequences are as obvious.

Peggy McIntosh, writing about systemic racism and white privilege, stated, "We need more understanding of the ways in which white "privilege" damages white people, for these are not the same ways in which it damages the victimized. Skewed white psyches are an inseparable part of the picture, though I do not want to confuse the kinds of damage done to the holders of special assets and to those who suffer the deficits. Many, perhaps most, of our white students in the United States think that racism doesn't affect them because they are not people of color; they do not see "whiteness" as a racial identity" (McIntosh, 1992). When you try to deny a person their humanity, understand that you cannot do so without diminishing your own.

When I was a child, my mother, a very religious woman, would frequently pray aloud that she wanted to live long enough until all seven of her children were old enough to know if they were being treated badly. I always thought this a curious prayer. But looking back from the perspective of a mother, I now understand that her prayer was that she would live until such time that her children were capable of asking for help if they were being mistreated. She did not want us to have to suffer in silence.

Black folks know when we are being treated unfairly, unfavorably, or unkindly. Oftentimes, we remain silent in order to keep the peace or to keep our jobs. For years, we have borne this burden by wearing the masks and presenting one face to white America and another to our brothers and sisters of color. While we may hold our tongue, with the exchange of a glance or the tilt of a head, we can silently convey to one another across a crowded room the fact that we see or hear the injustices playing out in our presence.

This silence has often been mistaken for ignorance, leading our offenders to the mistaken conclusion that we either don't know what is happening or have accepted with a grin and a shuffle our second-class citizenry.

1993

I don't think I'm prejudiced, but I am aware that the trusting spirit of the child that I once was has died. Now I search for indicators that I can trust—a smile, a sincere hello, maybe laugh lines around the eyes that tell me that the person has had numerous occasions to smile in this cold, hard world. Ironically, those indicators that I unconsciously seek as a reassurance of goodness are now routinely erased from the face of the bearer with skin stretched into unnatural tautness, erasing signs of kindness that were delicately etched into the skin.

Likewise, I believe that white folks know when they are being unfair and bestowing unearned favor on their own, but have come to expect that their behavior will go unquestioned and even supported by their fellow tribe members, whether family, friends, or employers. It appears that whites rarely have to worry about someone calling them out on their behavior because it serves to maintain the status quo of their tribe. During a recent conversation with a white male acquaintance, I was talking about how things needed to change. He asked with genuine sincerity, "Why would we change things?" Why, indeed? Empathy is one of life's kindest teachers, enabling us to learn life lessons without having to experience them firsthand. Accept the gift of empathy.

Despite all of the surface things that make us unique, at our core we are all more alike than different. We are born into this world. We love. We cry. We bleed red. We laugh. We die. In between our birth and death, we are all in the pursuit of our own brand of happiness, and looking for some meaning for our existence.

Hating one another is not the solution. To the white collective that are engaged in groupthink, pierce the bubble. Do not blithely be a part of the dissonance that is America, but rather commit yourself to working to help find a way to turn the tide. Be willing to stand up and speak out for what is right. Regardless of what you have been told to believe, know that the truth lies within your soul. Seek out the truth within you, and live your life from that place, for if you endeavor to live life fully awake and conscious, there will come a day of reckoning when you have to confront the person in the mirror.

Ways to Break Through to the Light:

- Question everything.
- Learn to trust what you feel.
- Be aware of the energy that you are putting out into the world.

- ➤ Become attuned to the energy that others emit.
- ➤ Understand that we are all interconnected.
- ➤ Understand that there is a reason that we are all unique individuals, and that there are lessons that we are to learn from one another.
- ➤ Don't allow your potential to be unrealized.
- ➤ Don't allow your talents to go unused.
- ➤ When you put your dreams out into the universe, don't try and dictate how they will materialize. Simply ask, give thanks, and get on with the business of doing the work.
- ➤ Follow a sincere apology with actions to right your wrongs.
- ➤ Forgiveness is difficult, keep working at it.
- ➤ Choose empathy.
- ➤ True friends are those who are willing to help you bear the weight of your pain. Be that friend to at least one individual.

Growing Out of the Fire

"Impossible is just a big word thrown around by small men who find it easier to live in the world they've been given, than to explore the power they have to change it."

— Muhammad Ali

In order for our nation to heal, we must all allow ourselves to feel the pain of our shared history.

Note to Self:

December 11, 2014

Father-God,

I look to you for guidance in regards to my writing. I want to help open minds by being honest and truthful but not by spreading hate. Guide me in the stories

to tell; the words to use in telling the stories, and may my words find their way to those whom they will help the most, regardless of their color. I am grateful, Father-God, for your perfect answer. I now release the problem as a problem and calmly and patiently observe the unfolding answers.
Dorothy

When I first heard about the church massacre in South Carolina, I was overcome with sadness, anger, and a deep weariness resulting not just from these particularly painful and unfathomable killings but, as succinctly tweeted by Christina Coleman, contributing editor of GlobalGrind.com, "Trauma after trauma after trauma after trauma with little time to heal." Suddenly…I couldn't breathe.

I went to work, against my initial judgment, and my sense of despair and loss was only deepened by the fact that at my workplace things went on as normal. No one paused to acknowledge to one another what had happened, to express any sorrow for the dying soul of our nation, to mourn the loss of our brethren. It was as if an execution in one of the few remaining sacred places left in the world had never happened.

A few days later as I stood watching the evening news, I listened in disbelief as one after the other, the family members of those nine innocent people whose lives had been callously snuffed out found within themselves love enough to extend to the killer forgiveness and prayers for salvation. Why weren't they angry? I asked myself. Why weren't they screaming to the heavens? Yet, each utterance of forgiveness loosened something hard and malignant that had lodged itself beneath my breastbone, and finally... I was able to exhale.

Later, I struggled to find words to articulate what I had experienced in that moment. President Obama said it best when, during the eulogy for the state senator and Reverend Clementa C. Pinckney, he declared, "Amazing grace. Amazing grace. Amazing grace."

Upon further reflection, I came to realize that what I had experienced could best be classified as what Jack Mezirow refers to as transformational learning brought about by a "disorienting dilemma" (Bierema, 2014). My disorienting dilemma of hearing the families' words of forgiveness led me to examine my own feelings of anger and assess my epistemological perspective and sociocultural and psychic assumptions. I realized that I was not alone in my feelings. I explored options for new roles and relationships and made plans for change. I continued acquiring skills and knowledge, trying new roles and building competence and self-confidence in new roles before finally reintegrating a new perspective into my life.

The above transformational learning experience transformed and broadened my focus. I went from wanting to help only my tribe to widening the scope of my tribe and, consequently, seeking to help a much larger tribe—the human tribe.

The following exercises were conceptualized to help start the process of healing, seeking forgiveness, and extending love.

Silent Confession

Think of those you have judged and placed within the constraints of a box of your making. Silently ask for their forgiveness for judging them without even knowing their journeys or their stories and vow to try to move through life without judgment but meeting all with an accepting and open heart.

Look at Me. See Me.

This exercise, much like the one presented above, deals with going below the surface of interacting with someone and really trying to get a glimpse of their soul. The exercise entails two individuals looking into each other's eyes. Again, no words are spoken, as the goal of the exercise is to provide an opportunity for the participants to really "see" the other individual.

The eyes are the windows of the soul, but we rarely have the courage to look deeply into someone's eyes. The act is too revealing, leaving us feeling exposed and vulnerable. It is hard to invest the time and emotional energy to try and see someone's true essence. This exercise will hopefully give learners the courage to at least make the attempt.

Silencing the Dogma and Assumptions

We have all heard of gratitude journals. I want to extend the act of journaling to include an exercise that can be cathartic and clarifying for the soul. In this "Silencing the Dogma and Assumptions" journal, write down thoughts of discomfort and judgment about those you consider the "Others" as they occur. Just get them out of your head and onto the paper unedited and unfiltered. Later, go back and spend some time writing about why you possibly felt the way you did, or thought the things that you did. Were your feelings valid, or were you just reacting to the hysteria and xenophobic reporting of the media?

We need to begin to deconstruct and question the origins of our assumptions and whether they hold true under close examination. James Zull (2006) noted that the gathering of data does not immediately lead to understanding. But reflection coupled with the act of embodied writing—taking an abstract idea and making it concrete—can further assist in the process of meaning making as we grapple with these new ideas and new ways of seeing the world.

I, like millions of Americans, consider myself a spiritual person rather than a religious person. What this means is that even though I grew up in the church, I am not currently a member of any church, nor do I attend church services. I do, however, believe in God. It continuously baffles me when people assume that just because I don't go to church, I do not have a relationship with God, and my soul is in dire need of saving. Also perplexing is the fact that there are so many religious people in our nation, and yet the deep racial divides still exist.

My relationship with God is personal, and I believe that prayers are sacred. I find myself praying and communing with God throughout the day regarding things both big and small. It calms me when things appear too large for me to handle or when the world just doesn't make any sense. So I pray and turn inward and go back, back as far as memory will take me, back as far as the spoken family history will take me, back further still to those memories that are embedded in my DNA to a knowingness that is innate and understood on a level deeper than the cellular and try to live life according to my soul's urgings.

It's easy to lose one's way in life. Part of the struggle is taking the time and having the courage to admit to yourself that you've wandered off course. Be brave. Take the first step. And remember, we will never be perfect people, but all that we can do is all that we can do. Then sit back and watch…

Dorothy L. Griggs

.

References

Bierema, Laura and Sharan Merriam. 2014. *Adult Learning Linking Theory and Practice*. San Francisco, CA: Jossey-Bass.

McIntosh, Peggy. 1992. "White privilege." *Creation Spirituality*, 33–35.

Zull, James E. 2006. "Key aspects of how the brain learns." *New Directions for Adult & Continuing Education, 2006* (110), 3–9. doi: 10.1002/ace.213

Dorothy L. Griggs

About the Author

Dorothy Griggs defines herself as a passionate writer, change agent, and cloud glazer. Through her writing she seeks to help individuals who are marginalized understand that they do not have to define themselves by other's limited version of them, as well as encourage honest and courageous dialogue among individuals interested in understanding how their silence and actions keep fertile the soil that breeds the continued marginalization of people who are different.

Dorothy holds a master's degree in educating adults from DePaul University, and her recent TEDxTalk/DePaul University titled, *Can You Cry for Me? Will You Cry with Me?* can be seen on YouTube. She is also the author and publisher of the novel, *Sisters in Spirit (An Old-School Love Story)*.